Unbelievable Pictures and Facts About Zimbabwe

By: Olivia Greenwood

Introduction

Zimbabwe is a country that is home to the famous Victoria Falls. It is also a country that has a vast history and culture. Today we will be exploring the truly fascinating country of Zimbabwe in more detail.

Do many people come to visit Zimbabwe?

Over the years Zimbabwe has become an increasingly popular country to visit. It is filled with many amazing tourist attractions.

Has the name of the country always been Zimbabwe?

No the name of the country has not always been the same. One of the most well-known previous names of the country is Rhodesia.

Will you find any national parks in the country?

You will find tons of massive national parks situated all over the country.

What items do they export from Zimbabwe?

Zimbabwe is a country that is actively involved in many exports. Some of the main items which they export include diamonds and raw tobacco.

What type of culture does Zimbabwe have?

Zimbabwe is known for being a country with a very mixed culture. There are all sorts of people from all different ethnicities who speak all different languages in Zimbabwe.

Will you find any mountains in Zimbabwe?

You will find many beautiful and exotic mountain ranges in the country of Zimbabwe.

Is Zimbabwe a big or small country?

The country of Zimbabwe is a really big country. It is certainly not a small country at all.

What kinds of food do they eat in the country?

The people in Zimbabwe eat lots of different foods. They enjoy eating maize, rice, and meats.

What type of landscape does Zimbabwe have?

Zimbabwe has a very unique landscape, it is filled with waterfalls, mountains, valleys and lots of wildlife.

Does Zimbabwe have its own national flower?

The country has its own national flower which goes by the name of Gloriosa superba.

Which city in Zimbabwe is the biggest city?

The biggest city in Zimbabwe is also the capital city, which is the city of Harare.

What languages do they speak in Zimbabwe?

Believe it or not, Zimbabwe has 16 official languages which are spoken in the country. Some of these languages include English, Ndau, Ndebele, Chewa, Xhosa and many more.

Which river in the country is the longest one?

Zimbabwe is filled with long rivers. The second biggest river in the country is called the Limpopo river. The longest river in the country is known as the Zambezi river.

Is Zimbabwe home to many animals?

The country is home to many wonderful animals. The country is known for the Big Five. This consists of the lion, rhinoceros, leopard, buffalo, and elephant.

Will you find an ocean in Zimbabwe?

You will not find any oceans in Zimbabwe. However, you will find many rivers and lakes.

Which sport do they play the most in Zimbabwe?

The sport which they love and play the most in Zimbabwe is soccer. This is regular football but they call it soccer.

Is it safe to travel in Zimbabwe?

It is safe to travel in most parts of Zimbabwe. Before you go to the country it is important to learn which places are safe and which places to avoid.

Where in the world will you find Zimbabwe?

Do you know how to find the continent of Africa on the map? This is where you will find the country of Zimbabwe. If you are having difficulty finding it, try looking for Zambia or Mozambique as they border Zimbabwe. You can also try and look for South Africa as it also borders the country.

Which city in Zimbabwe is the capital one?

Harare is the name of the capital city in Zimbabwe.

Is Zimbabwe a country that is landlocked?

The answer is yes. Zimbabwe is in fact, a country that is landlocked.

Made in the USA
Columbia, SC
12 March 2022

57554797R00024